Border Security in the 21st Century: Challenges and Solutions

Copyright Page

TITLE: Border Security in the 21st Century: Challenges and Solutions

1ST Edition

ISBN: 9798223328384

Border Security in the 21st Century: Challenges and Solutions

By Roberto Miguel Rodriguez

Chapter 1: Introduction to Border Security in the 21st Century

The Importance of Border Security

In recent years, the issue of border security has become increasingly critical, demanding the attention of politicians, think tank scholars, professors, teachers, students, authors, and scholars alike. This subchapter aims to highlight the significance of border security and its implications on various niches including emergency management, transportation security, maritime security, and immigration enforcement.

Border security serves as the first line of defense for any nation, safeguarding its citizens, economy, and sovereignty. With the rise of global terrorism, cross-border criminal activities, and illegal immigration, it is imperative that countries prioritize the protection of their borders. Politicians must recognize that an effective border security system is essential to maintaining national security and public safety.

One of the key aspects in understanding the importance of border security is its direct correlation with emergency management. In times of crisis, such as natural disasters or terrorist attacks, secure borders allow for efficient response and recovery efforts. By preventing unauthorized individuals or dangerous substances from entering the country, emergency management officials can focus their resources on addressing the immediate needs of the affected population.

Transportation security is another niche greatly impacted by border security measures. Enhanced border control ensures the safety of travelers and the integrity of transportation infrastructure. By effectively monitoring and regulating the movement of people and goods across borders, authorities can prevent the infiltration of contraband, drugs, and weapons into the transportation system. This, in turn, promotes efficient and secure trade, benefiting the national economy.

Maritime security, closely linked to border security, holds significant importance in coastal nations. By securing maritime borders, countries can combat piracy, drug trafficking, and illegal fishing. Additionally, effective border security measures enable the enforcement of maritime laws and regulations, protecting marine ecosystems and preserving national resources.

Lastly, border security plays a vital role in immigration enforcement. Striking a balance between facilitating legal immigration and deterring illegal immigration is crucial for any nation. By implementing robust border security measures, countries can ensure that immigration policies are followed, protecting the integrity of the immigration system and the rights of both citizens and migrants.

In conclusion, understanding the importance of border security is crucial for politicians, scholars, and professionals in the fields of emergency management, transportation security, maritime security, and immigration enforcement. A comprehensive and effective border security system is essential to protect national security, facilitate emergency response, promote economic growth, preserve marine resources, and ensure the integrity of immigration processes. By recognizing its significance, policymakers can work towards implementing innovative solutions that address the challenges of border security in the 21st century.

Evolution of Border Security Policies

Title: Evolution of Border Security Policies

Introduction:

In an increasingly interconnected world, the evolution of border security policies has become a critical subject for politicians, scholars, and professionals across various fields. As the book "Border Security in the 21st Century: Challenges and Solutions" delves into this complex topic, it aims to provide valuable insights to a diverse audience including politicians, think tank scholars, professors, teachers, students, authors, and scholars who specialize in border security, emergency management, transportation security, maritime security, and immigration enforcement. This subchapter specifically explores the historical development and transformation of border security policies, shedding light on the challenges and solutions that have emerged over time.

Historical Context:

The evolution of border security policies can be traced back to ancient civilizations, where walls and fortifications were erected to protect territories. However, in the 21st century, border security policies have become far more complex and multifaceted, driven by factors such as globalization, terrorism, mass migration, and trade expansion.

Early Approaches:

Initially, border security focused primarily on physical barriers and the deployment of personnel to deter unauthorized entry. However, these approaches proved inadequate as technology advanced and new threats emerged. This led to a shift towards intelligence-driven strategies that incorporated surveillance technologies, biometric identification systems, and data analysis to identify potential risks.

Globalization and Multilateral Cooperation:

The advent of globalization necessitated the development of border security policies that went beyond national borders. Collaboration between nations became vital to effectively combat transnational organized crime, human trafficking, and terrorism. This subchapter explores how international organizations, such as INTERPOL and the World Customs Organization, play a crucial role in promoting information sharing, harmonizing procedures, and fostering cooperation among nations.

Balancing Security and Facilitation:

A key challenge faced by policymakers is striking a balance between security measures and facilitating the movement of people and goods across borders. This subchapter examines the evolution of policies that aim to streamline trade and travel while maintaining robust security measures. Concepts like risk-based assessments, trusted traveler programs, and pre-clearance initiatives are explored as viable solutions.

Emerging Technologies:

Advancements in technology have revolutionized border security practices. From biometrics and facial recognition to drones and artificial intelligence, this subchapter discusses how these cutting-edge technologies are being integrated into border security frameworks to enhance detection capabilities, expedite processing, and improve overall security outcomes.

Conclusion:

As border security continues to evolve, policymakers, scholars, and professionals must remain vigilant and adaptable. By understanding the historical context, embracing multilateral cooperation, balancing security and facilitation, and harnessing the power of emerging technologies, effective solutions can be developed to address the ever-changing challenges of the 21st-century border landscape. This subchapter aims to equip the audience with a comprehensive understanding of the evolution of border security policies, inspiring further research, innovation, and collaboration in this crucial field.

Current Issues and Challenges

In the rapidly changing world of the 21st century, border security has emerged as a critical concern for nations worldwide. This subchapter explores the current issues and challenges that policymakers, scholars, and practitioners face in the field of border security. Addressing a diverse audience of politicians, think tank scholars, professors, teachers, students, authors, and scholars, this section aims to provide insights into the complex landscape of border security and its interconnectedness with emergency management, transportation security, maritime security, and immigration enforcement.

One of the foremost challenges in border security today is the increasing sophistication of transnational criminal organizations and terrorist networks. These groups exploit vulnerabilities in border management systems, using advanced technology and tactics to evade detection and smuggle illicit goods, drugs, and weapons across borders. This has necessitated a multi-faceted approach that combines intelligence-sharing, enhanced surveillance, and international cooperation to effectively counter these threats.

Another pressing issue is the management of mass migration and refugee flows. With the rise of conflicts, political instability, and climate-related disasters worldwide, millions of people are forced to flee their homes in search of safety and better opportunities. This places enormous strain on border security systems, as nations strive to balance humanitarian concerns with the need to protect their borders. Developing comprehensive and humane immigration policies, while ensuring effective border control, is a critical challenge that requires innovative solutions and international cooperation.

Emerging technologies such as drones, artificial intelligence, and biometrics pose both opportunities and challenges for border security. While these advancements have the potential to revolutionize border management and enhance security measures, they also raise concerns related to privacy, data protection, and ethical considerations. Policymakers and scholars must grapple with these issues to strike the right balance between security and individual rights.

The globalization of trade and travel has also presented unique challenges in securing transportation systems and maritime borders. Criminal networks exploit vulnerabilities in global supply chains, using legal trade channels to smuggle contraband or facilitate human trafficking. Strengthening cooperation between customs agencies, improving cargo screening technologies, and enhancing international standards are crucial to ensuring the security of global transportation networks.

In conclusion, the subchapter "Current Issues and Challenges" provides a comprehensive overview of the multifaceted problems faced by policymakers, scholars, and practitioners in the realm of border security. By addressing the concerns of politicians, think tank scholars, professors, teachers, students, authors, and scholars, this section aims to foster a deeper understanding of the complexities and interconnectedness of border security, emergency management, transportation security, maritime security, and immigration enforcement. By embracing innovative solutions, international cooperation, and a holistic approach, nations can navigate the ever-evolving landscape of border security in the 21st century.

Chapter 2: Border Security Policies and Strategies

Policy Frameworks for Border Security

Introduction:

Effective border security is crucial in the 21st century to address the numerous challenges and threats faced by nations around the world. This subchapter will delve into the policy frameworks that can be implemented to enhance border security. The content is specifically tailored to politicians, think tank scholars, professors, teachers, students, authors, and scholars interested in border security, emergency management, transportation security, maritime security, and immigration enforcement.

1. Comprehensive Border Security Strategies:

To ensure robust border security, a comprehensive approach is required. This entails implementing a multi-layered strategy that combines physical barriers, advanced technology, intelligence sharing, and cooperation with neighboring countries. Policy frameworks should emphasize the importance of integrating these elements to maximize effectiveness.

2. Risk-Based Approach:

Policy frameworks for border security should adopt a risk-based approach that focuses resources on high-risk areas and individuals. This approach allows for a more efficient allocation of limited resources, ensuring that security measures are targeted where they are most needed. Risk assessment tools, intelligence analysis, and data-driven decision-making should be at the core of such frameworks.

3. International Cooperation:

Border security is not solely a national concern but a global challenge. Policy frameworks should promote international cooperation and information sharing among nations to combat transnational threats effectively. Bilateral and multilateral agreements, joint operations, and intelligence sharing platforms should be established to foster collaboration and enhance border security efforts.

4. Interagency Coordination:

Effective border security requires seamless coordination among various agencies involved in border control, such as customs and border protection, immigration enforcement, law enforcement, intelligence agencies, and emergency management. Policy frameworks should emphasize the need for interagency collaboration, information sharing, and joint training exercises to enhance operational efficiency and effectiveness.

5. Public-Private Partnerships:

Recognizing the significance of public-private partnerships, policy frameworks should encourage collaboration between government agencies and the private sector. This cooperation can enhance border security through the deployment of innovative technologies, joint research and development, and sharing best practices. Incentives for private sector involvement and information sharing should be incorporated into the policy framework.

Conclusion:

The policy frameworks outlined above provide a foundation for enhancing border security in the 21st century. By adopting comprehensive strategies, risk-based approaches, international cooperation, interagency coordination, and public-private partnerships, nations can effectively address the challenges and threats associated with border security. It is crucial for politicians, think tank scholars, professors, teachers, students, authors, and scholars interested in border security, emergency management, transportation security, maritime security, and immigration enforcement to understand and advocate for these policy frameworks to promote a safer and more secure world.

International Cooperation and Collaboration

In today's interconnected world, the challenges of border security have become increasingly complex and require a coordinated and collaborative approach among nations. This subchapter explores the importance of international cooperation and collaboration in addressing the 21st-century challenges of border security.

Globalization and the advancement of technology have made it easier for criminals, terrorists, and smugglers to exploit vulnerabilities in border security systems. As a result, no single nation can effectively address these challenges alone. International cooperation and collaboration are crucial for sharing information, intelligence, and best practices, as well as for coordinating efforts to detect and deter threats at borders.

For politicians, the subchapter emphasizes the need to prioritize international cooperation and collaboration in their policies and decisions. By fostering diplomatic relations and partnerships with other nations, politicians can create a platform for information sharing, joint exercises, and capacity building initiatives. This can lead to the development of comprehensive border security strategies that are effective in preventing and responding to emerging threats.

Think tank scholars, professors, and authors play a vital role in conducting research and analysis on border security issues. This subchapter highlights the importance of their work in advocating for international cooperation and collaboration. By generating evidence-based policy recommendations, scholars and think tanks can influence decision-makers to prioritize cooperation and collaboration as a key component of border security strategies.

Teachers and students can benefit from understanding the significance of international cooperation and collaboration in the field of border security. By incorporating case studies and real-world examples into their curriculum, educators can help students grasp the complexities of border security challenges and the role of collaboration in addressing them. This knowledge will equip future leaders with the skills necessary to develop effective strategies and policies.

For scholars and professionals in the niches of emergency management, transportation security, maritime security, and immigration enforcement, this subchapter highlights the interdependencies and overlaps between their respective fields and border security. It emphasizes the need for cross-sectoral collaboration to address common challenges and enhance overall security.

In conclusion, international cooperation and collaboration are essential in addressing the challenges of border security in the 21st century. The subchapter aims to raise awareness among politicians, think tank scholars, professors, teachers, students, authors, and scholars about the importance of collaboration and provide them with insights into how they can contribute to fostering international cooperation in the field of border security. By working together, nations can effectively tackle border security challenges and ensure the safety and prosperity of their citizens in an increasingly interconnected world.

Role of Technology in Border Security

Title: Role of Technology in Border Security: Enhancing 21st Century Solutions

Introduction:

In the face of evolving threats and challenges in the 21st century, border security has become a critical concern for nations across the globe. This subchapter delves into the pivotal role that technology plays in bolstering border security efforts. Aimed at a diverse audience ranging from politicians and scholars to students and professionals in various niches, this section explores how technology is revolutionizing border security, emergency management, transportation security, maritime security, and immigration enforcement.

1. Border Security:

Advancements in technology have transformed the landscape of border security, enabling nations to protect their borders more effectively. Cutting-edge surveillance systems, such as drones and satellites, provide real-time monitoring of vast border regions, augmenting traditional manpower efforts. Biometric identification systems, including facial recognition and fingerprint scanning, enhance security measures by accurately verifying the identity of individuals crossing borders.

2. Emergency Management:

During times of crisis and emergencies, technology plays a crucial role in facilitating effective response and management. Integrated command and control systems leverage real-time data from various sources, enabling authorities to make informed decisions swiftly. Remote sensing technologies aid in identifying areas prone to natural disasters, helping authorities allocate resources and plan evacuation strategies.

3. Transportation Security:

In an era of increased global travel, technology is vital for ensuring transportation security. Advanced screening devices, such as full-body scanners and explosive detection systems, enhance security measures at airports, seaports, and land border crossings. Smart surveillance systems with facial recognition capabilities help identify potential threats and prevent unauthorized access to transportation hubs.

4. Maritime Security:

With a significant portion of global trade occurring through maritime routes, ensuring maritime security is of paramount importance. Satellite-based tracking systems and Automatic Identification Systems (AIS) allow authorities to monitor vessels in real-time, detecting any suspicious activities or unauthorized entries. Unmanned Surface Vessels (USVs) and underwater drones aid in conducting surveillance and inspections in maritime environments.

5. Immigration Enforcement:

Technology plays a crucial role in ensuring effective immigration enforcement while facilitating lawful travel. Biometric systems, including fingerprint and iris recognition, help verify the identity of travelers and identify individuals with criminal backgrounds or immigration violations. Advanced data analytics and information sharing platforms enable efficient processing and screening of travelers, ensuring compliance with immigration laws.

Conclusion:

As nations face evolving security challenges, harnessing the power of technology becomes imperative. This subchapter has provided an overview of how technology is shaping border security, emergency management, transportation security, maritime security, and immigration enforcement. By embracing innovative technological solutions, policymakers, scholars, and professionals in these niches can enhance their capabilities to secure borders, respond to emergencies, and safeguard their nations in the 21st century.

Chapter 3: Border Security Challenges and Threats

Transnational Organized Crime

One of the greatest challenges faced by border security agencies in the 21st century is the rise of transnational organized crime. This subchapter aims to shed light on the complex nature of this phenomenon and provide insights into the challenges and potential solutions for combating it effectively. Addressed to politicians, think tank scholars, professors, teachers, students, authors, and scholars within the niches of border security, emergency management, transportation security, maritime security, and immigration enforcement, this content will serve as a valuable resource for understanding the gravity of transnational organized crime and its implications for global security.

Transnational organized crime refers to criminal activities that span across national borders and involve organized groups with sophisticated networks and resources. These criminal enterprises operate across various sectors, ranging from drug trafficking, human smuggling, and arms smuggling to cybercrime, money laundering, and terrorism financing. Their activities pose significant threats not only to national security but also to global stability, as they undermine governance, erode the rule of law, and fuel violence and corruption.

In order to effectively combat transnational organized crime, it is crucial to understand its underlying causes and dynamics. Factors such as economic inequality, political instability, weak law enforcement and judicial systems, and porous borders contribute to the proliferation of these criminal networks. Additionally, advances in technology and communication have facilitated their operations, making it imperative for law enforcement agencies to adapt and develop innovative strategies to counter them.

Collaboration and cooperation among countries are essential in tackling transnational organized crime. Information-sharing platforms, intelligence exchanges, and joint operations are vital tools in disrupting these networks. Moreover, strengthening legal frameworks and enhancing the capacity of law enforcement agencies to investigate, prosecute, and dismantle these criminal organizations is of utmost importance. This requires investment in training, resources, and technology to ensure the effectiveness of these efforts.

Furthermore, addressing the root causes of transnational organized crime is crucial. This involves promoting economic development, fostering social inclusion, and improving governance in vulnerable regions. By reducing the incentives and opportunities for criminal activities, societies can mitigate the influence of these networks and create conditions for sustainable security and prosperity.

In conclusion, transnational organized crime is a grave challenge that demands a comprehensive and collaborative approach. This subchapter provides a comprehensive overview of the nature and impact of transnational organized crime, as well as strategies and solutions for countering it. By addressing the concerns of politicians, think tank scholars, professors, teachers, students, authors, and scholars within the niches of border security, emergency management, transportation security, maritime security, and immigration enforcement, this content aims to contribute to the ongoing dialogue on border security in the 21st century and help shape effective policies and practices in combating transnational organized crime.

Drug Trafficking and Smuggling

Introduction:

The illicit trade of drugs across national borders has become a pressing concern for governments and law enforcement agencies worldwide. The subchapter "Drug Trafficking and Smuggling" in the book "Border Security in the 21st Century: Challenges and Solutions" delves into the multifaceted nature of this global issue. Addressed to a diverse audience of politicians, think tank scholars, professors, teachers, students, authors, and scholars specializing in border security, emergency management, transportation security, maritime security, and immigration enforcement, this subchapter provides key insights into the challenges and potential solutions related to drug trafficking and smuggling.

Content:

1. The Global Drug Trade:

The subchapter begins by highlighting the magnitude of drug trafficking and smuggling, emphasizing its global reach and impact on societies. It discusses the economic, social, and political consequences of this illicit trade, drawing attention to its links with organized crime, violence, and corruption.

2. The Border Security Challenge:

This section explores the specific challenges faced by border security agencies in combating drug trafficking and smuggling. It discusses the vulnerabilities of transportation systems, border crossings, and maritime routes that criminals exploit to smuggle drugs across borders. It also examines the role of human traffickers and drug cartels in facilitating these illegal activities.

3. Innovative Technologies and Strategies:

To effectively tackle drug trafficking and smuggling, the subchapter highlights the importance of adopting innovative technologies and strategies. It explores the use of advanced surveillance systems, data analytics, and biometric tools to enhance border security and identify potential threats. It also emphasizes the significance of international cooperation and intelligence sharing among law enforcement agencies.

4. Strengthening Border Control:

This section focuses on the need to strengthen border control measures to counter drug trafficking. It highlights the significance of implementing robust inspection procedures, deploying trained personnel, and investing in modern detection equipment. It also discusses the importance of implementing effective risk assessment and targeting techniques to identify high-risk individuals and cargo.

5. Addressing the Root Causes:

Lastly, the subchapter delves into the importance of addressing the root causes of drug trafficking and smuggling. It emphasizes the need for comprehensive drug prevention and education programs, as well as the importance of social and economic development in regions affected by drug production and trafficking.

Conclusion:

The subchapter "Drug Trafficking and Smuggling" provides a comprehensive overview of the challenges and potential solutions related to this global issue. It aims to inform and engage a diverse audience of politicians, think tank scholars, professors, teachers, students, authors, and scholars with an interest in border security, emergency management, transportation security, maritime security, and immigration enforcement. By understanding the complexities of drug trafficking and smuggling, it is hoped that stakeholders can work together to develop effective strategies and policies to combat this illicit trade and create a safer and more secure world.

Human Trafficking and Illegal Immigration

Human trafficking and illegal immigration are two intertwined issues that pose significant challenges to border security in the 21st century. This subchapter delves into the complex relationship between these phenomena, addressing their implications and exploring potential solutions for policymakers, scholars, and professionals in the field.

Human trafficking, a form of modern-day slavery, involves the exploitation of individuals through force, fraud, or coercion for various purposes such as forced labor, sexual exploitation, or even organ trafficking. The illicit movement of people across borders provides traffickers with ample opportunities to exploit vulnerable individuals, making it crucial to address both human trafficking and illegal immigration comprehensively.

Illegal immigration often serves as a precursor to human trafficking, as individuals seeking better economic opportunities or fleeing conflict and persecution may fall into the hands of traffickers during their journey. The lack of legal means for migration and safe pathways incentivizes people to resort to unauthorized means, thereby exposing themselves to potential exploitation and abuse.

To effectively combat human trafficking and illegal immigration, a multifaceted approach is necessary. Strengthening border security is essential, as it acts as a deterrent and prevents unauthorized crossings. This includes deploying advanced surveillance technologies, increasing the number of border patrol agents, and enhancing cooperation between border agencies at national and international levels.

Additionally, addressing the root causes of illegal immigration is paramount. By promoting economic development, political stability, and social justice in countries of origin, potential migrants may be discouraged from embarking on perilous journeys. Engaging in international collaborations to disrupt human trafficking networks, dismantle smuggling operations, and provide support to victims is also crucial.

Education and awareness play a vital role in preventing human trafficking and illegal immigration. Targeting vulnerable populations with information campaigns that highlight the risks and consequences of unauthorized migration can help dissuade individuals from falling prey to traffickers. Equipping law enforcement officers, transportation security personnel, and emergency management officials with training on identifying and responding to trafficking situations is equally important.

In conclusion, human trafficking and illegal immigration are interconnected challenges that demand a comprehensive approach from policymakers, scholars, and professionals in the field of border security. By strengthening border control measures, addressing root causes, fostering international cooperation, and raising awareness, it is possible to mitigate the risks associated with these issues and protect vulnerable populations.

Target audience: politicians, think tank scholars, professors, teachers, students, authors, scholars

Niche: Border security, Emergency management, Transportation security, Maritime security, Immigration enforcement

Cybersecurity Threats at the Border

In today's interconnected world, where technology is becoming increasingly pervasive, the threats to border security have taken on a new dimension. The rise of cyber threats poses significant challenges to governments and law enforcement agencies responsible for safeguarding their nations' borders. This subchapter aims to shed light on the growing concerns surrounding cybersecurity threats at the border and the need for effective solutions.

The border, once defined solely by physical boundaries, has expanded to encompass the virtual domain. Cybercriminals and state-sponsored hackers exploit vulnerabilities in critical infrastructure, transportation systems, and immigration databases, compromising national security. These threats affect not only border security but also emergency management, transportation security, maritime security, and immigration enforcement.

Politicians, think tank scholars, professors, teachers, students, authors, and scholars must recognize the gravity of these cybersecurity threats and work collaboratively to address them. The first step is to understand the various forms of cyber threats that exist at the border. These include data breaches, ransomware attacks, identity theft, and the hacking of critical infrastructure systems.

The consequences of such breaches are multifaceted. For instance, compromised immigration databases can lead to the infiltration of terrorist networks, while attacks on transportation systems can disrupt the movement of goods and people, crippling national economies. Additionally, the compromise of maritime security systems can enable illicit activities such as drug trafficking and human smuggling.

To counter these threats effectively, a multi-layered approach is crucial. This involves enhancing cybersecurity infrastructure and capabilities, promoting cross-border cooperation, and fostering information sharing among relevant agencies. Governments should invest in robust cybersecurity measures, including advanced intrusion detection systems, encryption technologies, and cybersecurity training for personnel.

International collaboration is equally vital. Governments must establish agreements and protocols for sharing threat intelligence and coordinating cyber incident response. This can be achieved through bilateral or multilateral agreements, as well as participation in international organizations dedicated to cybersecurity cooperation.

Furthermore, public-private partnerships play a pivotal role in addressing cybersecurity threats at the border. Governments should engage with technology companies, academia, and research institutions to develop innovative solutions and stay ahead of evolving cyber threats. By fostering a collaborative environment, stakeholders can collectively tackle the challenges posed by cybercriminals.

In conclusion, the era of border security cannot be limited to physical boundaries alone. Cybersecurity threats have emerged as a significant concern, impacting various sectors such as emergency management, transportation security, maritime security, and immigration enforcement. Politicians, scholars, and professionals must recognize the urgency of addressing these threats and work together to develop comprehensive strategies that safeguard national security and maintain the integrity of border systems. By implementing a multi-layered approach, enhancing cybersecurity infrastructure, fostering international cooperation, and promoting public-private partnerships, we can effectively mitigate the risks associated with cybersecurity threats at the border.

Chapter 4: Border Security and Emergency Management

Emergency Preparedness at the Border

Emergency preparedness at the border is a critical aspect of ensuring the overall security and safety of a nation. As the world becomes increasingly interconnected, the challenges faced by border security agencies have become more complex. This subchapter aims to shed light on the importance of emergency preparedness at the border and the challenges and solutions that can be implemented to address them.

One of the primary goals of emergency preparedness at the border is to minimize the impact of potential threats and disasters. Whether it be natural disasters like hurricanes, floods, or earthquakes, or man-made emergencies such as terrorist attacks or pandemics, border security agencies must be well-equipped and trained to respond swiftly and effectively.

To achieve this, it is crucial for politicians, think tank scholars, professors, teachers, students, authors, and scholars to collaborate and develop comprehensive emergency response plans. These plans should consider the unique challenges posed by border security, emergency management, transportation security, maritime security, and immigration enforcement, which are all intricately interconnected.

An effective emergency preparedness plan at the border must involve timely information sharing, coordination, and cooperation among various agencies responsible for border security. This includes law enforcement agencies, immigration authorities, customs and border protection, transportation security agencies, and emergency management organizations.

Furthermore, it is imperative to invest in research and development to enhance technological capabilities in border security and emergency management. Advanced surveillance systems, sensors, and communication networks can significantly enhance situational awareness and enable swift response during emergencies.

Training and capacity building programs for border security personnel should be prioritized. These programs should include comprehensive training in emergency response protocols, crisis management, and coordination with international partners. Cross-border cooperation and information-sharing mechanisms should be established to ensure a coordinated response during emergencies that transcend national borders.

In conclusion, emergency preparedness at the border is a vital component of overall national security. The challenges faced by border security agencies in the 21st century require innovative solutions and comprehensive planning. By fostering collaboration among politicians, scholars, and professionals in the fields of border security, emergency management, transportation security, maritime security, and immigration enforcement, nations can better prepare for and respond to emergencies at the border. Through investments in technology, training, and international cooperation, we can ensure the safety and security of our borders while effectively managing emergencies that may arise.

Border Security and Natural Disasters

In recent years, the world has witnessed an increase in the frequency and intensity of natural disasters, ranging from hurricanes and floods to wildfires and earthquakes. These catastrophic events have not only posed significant challenges to emergency management and disaster response efforts but have also highlighted the crucial role of border security in mitigating their impact and ensuring the safety and well-being of affected populations. This subchapter explores the intersection of border security and natural disasters, shedding light on the challenges faced and proposing innovative solutions to address them.

One of the key challenges in the context of natural disasters is the efficient mobilization of resources and personnel across borders. During emergencies, it is essential to facilitate the rapid deployment of emergency response teams, search and rescue operations, and the transportation of essential supplies and equipment. However, existing border security protocols and immigration enforcement measures can often hinder the swift movement of these resources. This necessitates the development of flexible and adaptive border security frameworks that prioritize the expedited entry and exit of emergency personnel and aid materials while maintaining necessary security checks.

Furthermore, the issue of maritime security gains particular significance in the context of natural disasters, as coastal regions are often the most vulnerable to such events. Enhancing maritime security measures, including the monitoring of maritime traffic, strengthening port security, and improving communication and coordination among coastal states, is crucial to effectively respond to and mitigate the impact of natural disasters. Additionally, investing in advanced technologies such as remote sensing and early warning systems can significantly enhance maritime security capabilities, allowing for timely and targeted disaster response efforts.

Another aspect that deserves attention is the integration of transportation security and border security in disaster management. Transportation infrastructure plays a critical role in facilitating the movement of goods, services, and people during emergencies. Robust transportation security measures, including the protection of critical transportation infrastructure and the establishment of contingency plans, are essential to ensure the uninterrupted flow of resources and personnel. Moreover, the seamless coordination between transportation security agencies and border security authorities is vital to prevent the exploitation of disaster situations by illicit actors.

In conclusion, the nexus between border security and natural disasters poses unique challenges that require innovative solutions. By prioritizing the facilitation of emergency response efforts, enhancing maritime security capabilities, and integrating transportation security measures, governments can effectively address these challenges and ensure the safety and well-being of their populations during times of crisis. This subchapter provides a comprehensive overview of the issues at hand and offers recommendations for policymakers, scholars, and practitioners in the fields of border security, emergency management, transportation security, maritime security, and immigration enforcement.

Crisis Response and Recovery

In the face of evolving threats and increasing security challenges, effective crisis response and recovery measures are essential for maintaining border security in the 21st century. This subchapter explores the strategies, challenges, and solutions associated with crisis response and recovery in the context of border security. It aims to provide valuable insights to a diverse audience, including politicians, think tank scholars, professors, teachers, students, authors, and scholars, who are engaged in various niches such as border security, emergency management, transportation security, maritime security, and immigration enforcement.

1. Understanding the Nature of Crisis: This section delves into the various types of crises that can impact border security, including natural disasters, terrorist attacks, pandemics, and organized crime. It highlights the importance of comprehensive risk assessments and the need for proactive planning and preparedness to effectively respond to and recover from these crises.

2. Crisis Response Strategies: This section explores a range of crisis response strategies, including the establishment of multi-agency coordination mechanisms, leveraging technology and data analytics for real-time monitoring, and enhancing interagency cooperation at national and international levels. It emphasizes the significance of a coordinated and integrated approach to crisis response, involving all relevant stakeholders.

3. Recovery and Resilience: Building on effective crisis response, this section emphasizes the importance of recovery and resilience in border security. It highlights the need for comprehensive recovery plans that address not only the immediate aftermath of a crisis but also focus on long-term rehabilitation, infrastructure reconstruction, and community reintegration. Additionally, it discusses the role of resilience in preventing future crises and strengthening border security systems.

4. Lessons Learned and Best Practices: Drawing upon real-world examples and case studies, this section analyzes the lessons learned from past crises and identifies best practices in crisis response and recovery. It examines successful initiatives implemented in different countries and regions, highlighting their effectiveness and relevance in the context of border security.

By addressing the intricacies of crisis response and recovery in the realm of border security, this subchapter aims to equip the audience with the knowledge and tools necessary to navigate the complex challenges of the 21st century. It emphasizes the importance of proactive planning, interagency collaboration, and comprehensive recovery strategies to ensure the resilience and effectiveness of border security systems in the face of evolving threats.

Chapter 5: Transportation Security and Border Crossings

Securing Airports and Seaports

In today's interconnected world, border security has become a critical concern for nations around the globe. The challenges faced by countries in managing their borders have evolved significantly, necessitating innovative solutions to ensure the safety and integrity of their citizens and infrastructure. One of the key areas that demand utmost attention is securing airports and seaports, as they serve as crucial gateways for international travel and trade.

Airports have long been recognized as potential targets for terrorist attacks due to the high volume of passengers and the complex operations involved in managing air traffic. Therefore, it is imperative for governments to implement comprehensive security measures to safeguard these vital transportation hubs. This subchapter explores the challenges faced in securing airports and presents effective solutions to address these concerns.

First and foremost, enhancing passenger screening procedures is of paramount importance. Advanced technologies, such as full-body scanners, biometric identification systems, and explosive detection devices, should be deployed to detect any potential threats. Additionally, the training of security personnel should be rigorous, ensuring that they are well-equipped to handle any security breach effectively.

Furthermore, seaports serve as key entry points for a significant portion of international trade and are an essential part of a country's economic infrastructure. Securing seaports involves a unique set of challenges, given the vastness of water bodies and the extensive range of vessels that dock at these ports. Governments must invest in advanced surveillance systems, including radar and sonar technologies, to monitor maritime activities effectively. Additionally, implementing strict access control measures, such as mandatory identification checks and background screenings for port workers, can help mitigate security risks.

It is crucial for policymakers to recognize that securing airports and seaports goes beyond physical measures alone. Collaboration among various stakeholders, including government agencies, law enforcement bodies, and private sector entities, is essential. Information sharing and coordination among these entities should be streamlined to ensure a cohesive approach to border security.

In conclusion, securing airports and seaports is a critical aspect of border security in the 21st century. Effective measures must be implemented to address the specific challenges faced in these areas. By leveraging advanced technologies, enhancing screening procedures, and fostering collaboration among stakeholders, governments can strengthen the safety and resilience of their transportation infrastructure, thereby ensuring the well-being of their citizens and the smooth flow of goods and people across borders.

Land Transportation Security Measures

In today's interconnected world, ensuring the safety and security of land transportation is of utmost importance. With the movement of goods, people, and vehicles across borders, it is crucial to implement effective land transportation security measures. This subchapter aims to shed light on the challenges faced in this area and propose potential solutions for policymakers and stakeholders.

Border security is a complex issue that requires a multi-faceted approach. Enhanced screening procedures should be implemented at border checkpoints to detect potential threats and prevent illegal activities. The use of advanced scanning technologies, such as X-ray scanners and explosive detection systems, can help identify hidden contraband and dangerous materials. Additionally, the deployment of trained security personnel and the use of biometric identification systems can further enhance security at border crossings.

Emergency management plays a vital role in land transportation security. Preparedness and response plans should be developed to address various emergency scenarios, including natural disasters, terrorist attacks, and accidents. Regular drills and exercises can help ensure that emergency procedures are well-coordinated and effective. Collaboration between relevant agencies, such as law enforcement, emergency services, and transportation authorities, is essential to enable a swift response and minimize the impact of emergencies.

Transportation security extends beyond border checkpoints. Measures should be implemented throughout the entire transportation network, including highways, railways, and bus terminals. Surveillance systems, including CCTV cameras and license plate recognition technology, can help monitor and deter criminal activities. Furthermore, the use of intelligent transportation systems can enhance traffic management and provide real-time information to authorities, enabling them to respond quickly to any security threats.

Maritime security also plays a significant role in land transportation security. Ports and harbors are vital hubs for international trade, and ensuring their security is crucial. Implementing stringent access control measures, enhancing cargo screening procedures, and increasing the presence of maritime security forces can help prevent the smuggling of contraband and illicit activities.

Effective land transportation security measures should also consider immigration enforcement. Proper documentation, visa screening, and biometric verification can help identify and deter individuals with malicious intent. Cooperation between immigration agencies and transportation authorities is essential to ensure that immigration laws are enforced effectively without hindering the movement of legitimate travelers.

In conclusion, land transportation security measures are critical in maintaining the safety and integrity of borders and transportation networks. Policymakers and stakeholders must work together to implement comprehensive solutions that address the challenges posed by border security, emergency management, transportation security, maritime security, and immigration enforcement. By adopting advanced technologies, enhancing coordination between agencies, and promoting international cooperation, we can create a secure and efficient land transportation system for the 21st century.

Challenges and Solutions for International Transportation

In today's interconnected world, international transportation plays a vital role in facilitating trade, fostering economic growth, and promoting cultural exchange. However, it also presents various challenges that demand effective solutions to ensure the smooth flow of goods and people across borders. This subchapter will explore the key challenges faced in international transportation and propose viable solutions to address them.

One of the foremost challenges in international transportation is border security. As borders become increasingly porous, the risk of smuggling illicit goods, trafficking, and terrorism poses a significant threat. To combat this, policymakers must prioritize the implementation of advanced technologies such as biometric identification, surveillance systems, and data analytics. These tools can enhance border control efficiency while minimizing disruptions to legitimate travelers and trade.

Additionally, emergency management in international transportation is crucial. Natural disasters, pandemics, and other unforeseen events can severely disrupt transportation networks, causing significant economic and humanitarian consequences. Governments and international organizations should collaborate to develop comprehensive contingency plans, establish early warning systems, and invest in infrastructure resilience to mitigate the impact of such emergencies.

Another pressing challenge is transportation security. With the increasing sophistication of cyber threats, ensuring the safety of critical infrastructure and transportation systems is paramount. Governments must invest in robust cybersecurity measures, promote information sharing between public and private entities, and conduct regular vulnerability assessments to identify and address potential weaknesses.

Maritime security is a specific area of concern within international transportation. Piracy, illegal fishing, and drug trafficking pose significant risks to maritime trade routes. Enhanced international cooperation, increased maritime patrols, and the establishment of secure ports are essential to safeguarding maritime transportation and ensuring the uninterrupted flow of goods.

Lastly, immigration enforcement remains a contentious issue in international transportation. Striking a balance between facilitating legitimate travel and controlling illegal migration is a complex task. Governments should invest in modernizing border infrastructure, enhancing visa processing systems, and implementing effective screening procedures to identify potential security threats while expediting the movement of legitimate travelers.

In conclusion, addressing the challenges in international transportation requires a multi-faceted approach. Policymakers need to prioritize border security, emergency management, transportation security, maritime security, and immigration enforcement. By embracing advanced technologies, promoting international cooperation, and investing in infrastructure resilience, we can ensure the safe and efficient movement of goods and people across borders. This, in turn, will foster economic growth, enhance cultural exchange, and contribute to a more secure and prosperous world.

Chapter 6: Maritime Security and Border Surveillance

Securing Coastal Borders and Ports

Introduction:

In the interconnected world of the 21st century, border security has become a top priority for nations across the globe. This subchapter delves into the critical aspect of securing coastal borders and ports, which are essential for the overall defense and economic prosperity of a nation. Addressing the concerns of politicians, think tank scholars, professors, teachers, students, authors, and scholars, this chapter offers insights into the challenges and solutions involved in coastal border and port security. It explores the intersections of border security, emergency management, transportation security, maritime security, and immigration enforcement.

The Importance of Coastal Borders and Ports:

Coastal borders and ports are vital gateways for trade, tourism, and transportation. However, they also pose significant security risks, making them attractive targets for illicit activities such as drug trafficking, human smuggling, and terrorism. Therefore, it is imperative to implement robust security measures to safeguard these areas effectively.

Challenges in Securing Coastal Borders and Ports:

Securing coastal borders and ports presents unique challenges due to their vast expanse, complex geography, and diverse maritime environment. This subchapter analyzes these challenges and provides a comprehensive understanding of the complexities involved. It explores issues such as limited resources, jurisdictional overlaps, technological advancements, and the need for interagency cooperation.

Solutions and Best Practices:

To overcome these challenges, effective solutions and best practices must be implemented. This subchapter explores a range of strategies, including advanced surveillance systems, intelligence sharing, risk assessment methodologies, interagency collaboration, and public-private partnerships. It also highlights successful case studies from around the world, showcasing innovative approaches to coastal border and port security.

The Role of Emergency Management and Immigration Enforcement:

Coastal borders and ports can be vulnerable to natural disasters, such as hurricanes, tsunamis, and oil spills. This subchapter emphasizes the importance of integrating emergency management protocols into the security framework. Additionally, it discusses the crucial role of immigration enforcement in preventing unauthorized entry and managing the flow of people across coastal borders and ports.

Conclusion:

Securing coastal borders and ports requires a comprehensive and multifaceted approach. This subchapter provides valuable insights for politicians, think tank scholars, professors, teachers, students, authors, and scholars interested in border security, emergency management, transportation security, maritime security, and immigration enforcement. By understanding the challenges and implementing effective solutions, nations can ensure the safety, prosperity, and resilience of their coastal borders and ports in the 21st century.

Maritime Terrorism and Piracy

Maritime Terrorism and Piracy: Protecting the Seas in the 21st Century

Introduction

As globalization continues to shape our world, maritime security has emerged as a critical concern for nations around the globe. The rise of maritime terrorism and piracy poses multifaceted challenges that demand immediate attention and effective solutions. This subchapter delves into the complexities of these issues and explores the strategies required to safeguard our seas and ensure the safety of maritime trade, transportation, and border security.

Understanding Maritime Terrorism

Maritime terrorism refers to acts of violence or criminal activities perpetrated on the high seas or within maritime territories, with the aim of causing political, economic, or social disruption. These acts are carried out by both state-sponsored and non-state actors, posing a severe threat to national security and global stability. The accessibility, vastness, and interconnectedness of the world's oceans make them attractive targets for terrorist organizations seeking to exploit vulnerabilities in maritime infrastructure.

The Challenge of Piracy

While piracy may conjure images of the past, it remains a significant challenge in the 21st century. Modern piracy threatens the safety of seafarers, disrupts global trade, and undermines economic development in coastal regions. Piracy hotspots such as the Gulf of Aden, the Strait of Malacca, and the Niger Delta require heightened attention and cooperation among nations to combat this menace effectively.

Solutions for Maritime Security

Addressing maritime terrorism and piracy requires a comprehensive and cooperative approach. Governments, international organizations, and industry stakeholders must collaborate to enhance intelligence sharing, strengthen law enforcement capabilities, and promote regional cooperation. Investing in technological advancements such as satellite surveillance, automated identification systems, and unmanned aerial vehicles can significantly enhance maritime domain awareness and enable rapid response to emerging threats.

Additionally, capacity building and training programs for local law enforcement agencies and coast guards are crucial in strengthening border security and emergency management capabilities. International agreements, frameworks, and conventions, such as the United Nations Convention on the Law of the Sea, serve as critical tools for addressing maritime security challenges and ensuring cross-border cooperation.

Conclusion

Maritime terrorism and piracy pose complex challenges to global security, necessitating a coordinated response from all stakeholders. By embracing innovative technologies, fostering international cooperation, and investing in capacity building, nations can effectively combat these threats. Policymakers, think tank scholars, professors, teachers, students, authors, and scholars must engage in multidisciplinary discussions and research to develop comprehensive strategies that protect our seas, support trade and transportation, and safeguard national borders. Only through collaborative efforts can we secure the maritime domain and ensure a safer and more prosperous future for all.

Surveillance and Monitoring Technologies

In the 21st century, the challenges faced by border security, emergency management, transportation security, maritime security, and immigration enforcement have become more complex than ever before. To effectively address these challenges, it is crucial to leverage the power of innovative surveillance and monitoring technologies. This subchapter explores the advancements in these technologies and their potential impact on the aforementioned niches.

One of the most significant developments in surveillance technology is the use of drones or unmanned aerial vehicles (UAVs). Drones equipped with high-resolution cameras and thermal imaging sensors can provide real-time monitoring of vast border areas, enhancing border security efforts. Furthermore, these UAVs can be deployed in emergency management to gather crucial data during natural disasters or search and rescue missions. The ability to swiftly deploy drones in these situations can significantly improve response times and save lives.

Another vital aspect of surveillance and monitoring technologies is the use of advanced sensors and biometrics. These tools allow for the detection and identification of potential threats, such as illegal immigrants or dangerous cargo, in transportation and maritime security. Biometric systems, including fingerprint and facial recognition, enable quick and accurate identification, reducing the risk of human error and enhancing efficiency in immigration enforcement.

The rise of the Internet of Things (IoT) has also revolutionized surveillance and monitoring. By connecting various devices, such as cameras, sensors, and access control systems, through a network, security agencies can create a comprehensive and interconnected surveillance infrastructure. This infrastructure can provide real-time data analysis, alert systems, and predictive analytics, further enhancing the effectiveness of border security, emergency management, transportation security, maritime security, and immigration enforcement.

However, it is essential to balance the benefits of surveillance and monitoring technologies with privacy concerns. As policymakers, politicians, and scholars, it is crucial to establish robust frameworks and regulations that protect individual privacy rights while harnessing the potential of these technologies. Transparency, accountability, and regular audits should be implemented to ensure that surveillance activities are conducted within legal boundaries.

In conclusion, surveillance and monitoring technologies have emerged as powerful tools in addressing the challenges faced by border security, emergency management, transportation security, maritime security, and immigration enforcement. Drones, advanced sensors and biometrics, and IoT have the potential to enhance situational awareness, improve response times, and facilitate accurate threat detection. However, it is crucial to strike a balance between the benefits of these technologies and individual privacy rights. By embracing these advancements responsibly, policymakers, scholars, and other stakeholders can pave the way for a safer and more secure future.

Chapter 7: Immigration Enforcement and Border Control

Immigration Policies and Border Control

Introduction:

In the 21st century, the challenges posed by border security have become increasingly complex and multifaceted. With the rise in globalization, the movement of people across borders has increased significantly, leading to a range of economic, social, and security implications. This subchapter explores the various immigration policies and border control measures that policymakers and authorities can adopt to address these challenges effectively.

Understanding the Need for Immigration Policies:

Immigration policies play a crucial role in managing the influx of people across borders. They not only regulate the entry and exit of individuals but also shape the socio-economic fabric of nations. Effective immigration policies should strike a balance between promoting economic growth, protecting national security, and respecting humanitarian concerns.

Border Control Measures:

1. Enhanced Surveillance and Technology:

Investing in advanced surveillance systems, such as drones, satellites, and biometric identification, can significantly enhance border control efforts. These technologies can help monitor and detect illegal activities at the borders, ensuring greater security and efficiency.

2. Strengthening Border Patrol and Personnel:

Increasing the number of border patrol agents and equipping them with adequate resources, training, and technology is vital for effective border control. This ensures a strong presence at the borders and enables timely response to any security threats or breaches.

3. Collaborative Approaches:

Developing partnerships and cooperation with neighboring countries is crucial in addressing the challenges of border security and immigration. Sharing intelligence, joint operations, and coordinated efforts can help prevent illegal immigration and transnational crime.

4. Streamlined Immigration Processes:

Efficient immigration processing systems can help mitigate the risks associated with illegal immigration. Simplifying visa procedures, implementing electronic travel authorization systems, and utilizing biometric identification can expedite lawful entry while maintaining security.

5. Humanitarian Considerations:

Policies should also account for humanitarian concerns, including asylum seekers and refugees. Establishing fair and efficient processes for granting asylum, ensuring humane treatment, and providing necessary support can uphold international obligations and foster a compassionate approach to immigration.

Conclusion:

Effective immigration policies and robust border control measures are essential for maintaining national security, facilitating economic growth, and upholding humanitarian values. Policymakers, scholars, and security experts must work together to strike the right balance between security and openness, ensuring that border security measures align with the evolving challenges of the 21st century. By adopting collaborative, technology-driven, and humanitarian-focused approaches, nations can successfully manage immigration and border control in an ever-changing global landscape.

Detention and Deportation Procedures

Introduction:

Detention and deportation procedures are crucial aspects of border security and immigration enforcement. In an era where global migration patterns are constantly evolving, it is imperative to have effective mechanisms in place to manage and regulate the movement of people across borders. This subchapter will delve into the complexities surrounding detention and deportation, exploring the challenges and potential solutions within the context of border security in the 21st century.

Understanding Detention:

Detention serves as a temporary measure to ensure the proper processing and screening of individuals who have crossed international borders. However, the detention of migrants, especially vulnerable populations such as children and families, has sparked considerable debate. This section will examine the humanitarian and legal dimensions of detention, assessing the balance between national security concerns and human rights obligations.

Deportation Procedures:

Deportation, or the removal of individuals from a country, is an integral part of immigration enforcement. However, the implementation of deportation policies can be complex and contentious. This section will explore the various procedures involved in deportation, including legal frameworks, administrative processes, and the role of immigration courts. It will also address the challenges of deporting individuals with criminal records, assessing the potential risks and benefits associated with different approaches.

Challenges and Solutions:

Detention and deportation procedures face numerous challenges in the 21st century. This section will discuss the difficulties presented by large-scale migration flows, the need for effective information sharing between countries, and the importance of cooperation between immigration enforcement agencies. Furthermore, it will examine the potential solutions to enhance efficiency, fairness, and transparency in detention and deportation processes, including the use of technology, alternative forms of detention, and community-based alternatives to deportation.

Conclusion:

Detention and deportation procedures play a critical role in maintaining border security and enforcing immigration laws. However, these processes must be conducted in a manner that respects human rights and upholds international obligations. This subchapter has explored the multidimensional aspects of detention and deportation, highlighting the challenges faced in the 21st century. By considering innovative solutions and fostering international cooperation, policymakers, scholars, and practitioners can work together to develop more effective and humane approaches to detention and deportation, ensuring the integrity of border security while respecting individual rights and dignity.

Border Control and Human Rights

Introduction:

The intersection of border control and human rights is an essential topic in today's global landscape. As countries strive to enhance their border security measures, it is crucial to address the potential implications on human rights. This subchapter will explore the challenges and solutions associated with balancing border control efforts while respecting the fundamental rights of individuals.

Understanding the Dilemma:

Border security is a pressing concern for politicians, think tank scholars, professors, teachers, students, authors, and scholars in various niches like border security, emergency management, transportation security, maritime security, and immigration enforcement. However, the enforcement of border control measures should not infringe upon the human rights of individuals, including migrants, refugees, and asylum seekers.

The Impact on Human Rights:

Enhanced border security measures can inadvertently lead to the violation of human rights. Excessive use of force, arbitrary detention, and discrimination can occur, raising concerns about the dignity and wellbeing of individuals. The right to seek asylum, the prohibition of torture, and non-refoulement are among the critical human rights principles that must be upheld.

Balancing Security and Human Rights:

It is essential to strike a balance between effective border control and the protection of human rights. This can be achieved through the implementation of comprehensive policies that prioritize both aspects. Investing in technology and intelligence can enhance border security while reducing the need for invasive measures. Transparent and accountable border control practices should be established to prevent abuses and ensure the fair treatment of individuals.

International Cooperation:

Addressing border security challenges requires international cooperation. Collaboration between countries can facilitate the exchange of best practices, intelligence sharing, and capacity building. Furthermore, promoting dialogue and understanding among nations can help prevent the demonization of migrants and foster a more compassionate approach to border control.

Improving Immigration Processes:

One way to address the border control and human rights dilemma is by improving immigration processes. Establishing efficient and fair asylum procedures, creating legal pathways for migration, and providing support for integration can reduce the need for individuals to resort to irregular and dangerous routes. By addressing the root causes of migration, such as poverty and violence, countries can contribute to more humane border control practices.

Conclusion:

Border control and human rights are intricately linked, and striking the right balance between the two is crucial. Policymakers, scholars, and practitioners in the fields of border security, emergency management, transportation security, maritime security, and immigration enforcement must prioritize human rights while implementing effective border control measures. International cooperation, improved immigration processes, and transparent practices can contribute to a more secure and rights-respecting border management approach in the 21st century.

Chapter 8: Enhancing Border Security through Technology

Biometric Systems and Identification Technologies

In today's rapidly evolving world, border security, emergency management, transportation security, maritime security, and immigration enforcement have become critical issues for governments worldwide. The challenges faced in these areas require innovative and effective solutions to ensure the safety and well-being of nations and their citizens. One such solution lies in the use of biometric systems and identification technologies.

Biometric systems are cutting-edge tools that utilize unique physical or behavioral characteristics of individuals to establish their identity. By leveraging these technologies, governments can enhance security measures and streamline identification processes at various checkpoints. This subchapter explores the potential of biometric systems and identification technologies in addressing the challenges faced by border security, emergency management, transportation security, maritime security, and immigration enforcement.

Biometric systems offer several advantages over traditional identification methods. They provide a highly accurate and reliable means of authentication, reducing the risk of identity fraud and unauthorized access. Additionally, biometric technologies are non-intrusive and can be seamlessly integrated into existing infrastructure, making them user-friendly and efficient.

For border security, biometric systems can play a pivotal role in preventing illegal immigration and transnational crime. Facial recognition, iris scanning, and fingerprinting can facilitate quick and accurate identification of individuals, allowing authorities to detect and apprehend potential threats effectively. Furthermore, these systems can be integrated with databases of known criminals and terrorists, enabling real-time identification and tracking of suspects.

In the realm of emergency management, biometric systems can aid in disaster response and recovery efforts. By registering biometric data of residents, authorities can quickly locate and assist individuals during emergencies, ensuring timely evacuation and provision of aid. Biometric systems can also help in identifying missing persons and reuniting families in the aftermath of a crisis.

Transportation security can be significantly enhanced through the use of biometric systems. Biometric authentication can be employed at airports, seaports, and train stations, enabling seamless and secure movement of passengers. This technology can also be integrated with watch lists and databases to identify individuals with potential threats, preventing them from traveling undetected.

Maritime security can benefit from biometric systems by enabling secure access control to ships and ports, preventing unauthorized personnel from gaining entry. Biometric data can be used to authenticate crew members, ensuring the safety and integrity of maritime operations.

In immigration enforcement, biometric systems can streamline the identification and verification processes for visa applicants and border crossers. By collecting biometric data, authorities can accurately determine the identity and background of individuals, reducing the risk of fraudulent entries and enhancing border control.

In conclusion, biometric systems and identification technologies offer immense potential in addressing the challenges faced in border security, emergency management, transportation security, maritime security, and immigration enforcement. By leveraging these advanced tools, governments can enhance their capabilities in ensuring the safety and security of their nations. It is imperative for policymakers, scholars, and professionals in these fields to explore and embrace the possibilities offered by biometric systems to build a safer and more secure future.

Surveillance and Monitoring Systems

In the ever-evolving landscape of border security, the role of surveillance and monitoring systems has become increasingly crucial. This subchapter aims to shed light on the existing challenges and potential solutions related to these systems, addressing the specific concerns of politicians, think tank scholars, professors, teachers, students, authors, and scholars who specialize in border security, emergency management, transportation security, maritime security, and immigration enforcement.

Border security is a paramount concern for nations worldwide. As borders become more porous and threats become more sophisticated, it is imperative to employ robust surveillance and monitoring systems. These systems should be able to track and identify potential threats, ranging from illegal border crossings to the smuggling of contraband materials.

One of the primary challenges faced in implementing effective surveillance and monitoring systems is the vastness of border areas. A comprehensive solution requires a combination of technologies such as radar, sonar, unmanned aerial vehicles (UAVs), and satellite imagery. These systems can provide real-time data, allowing authorities to respond swiftly and effectively to potential threats.

However, the implementation of such systems often requires significant financial investments. This is where the role of politicians becomes crucial. They must advocate for increased funding and support for research and development in border security technologies. Additionally, think tank scholars can contribute by conducting in-depth studies on the cost-effectiveness and impact of various surveillance and monitoring systems.

Another critical aspect to consider is emergency management. Surveillance and monitoring systems can aid in disaster response and recovery efforts. By monitoring border areas, authorities can quickly identify and respond to natural disasters, terrorist attacks, or other emergencies. This requires coordination between various agencies, including emergency management personnel, law enforcement, and intelligence agencies. Professors, teachers, and students can contribute by designing comprehensive training programs that equip personnel with the necessary skills to handle emergencies effectively.

Transportation security and maritime security are also essential niches that benefit from surveillance and monitoring systems. By integrating these systems into ports, airports, and other transportation hubs, authorities can enhance security measures, detect smuggling attempts, and identify potential threats in cargo shipments. Scholars specializing in transportation security and maritime security can contribute by analyzing the effectiveness of these systems and proposing innovative solutions.

Lastly, immigration enforcement is an area where surveillance and monitoring systems play a significant role. By monitoring border areas and immigration checkpoints, authorities can prevent illegal immigration, identify human trafficking operations, and apprehend individuals with criminal backgrounds. Authors and scholars can contribute by analyzing the ethical implications of these systems and proposing policies that balance security concerns with human rights considerations.

In conclusion, surveillance and monitoring systems are indispensable tools in modern-day border security. To address the challenges and find effective solutions, collaboration between politicians, think tank scholars, professors, teachers, students, authors, and scholars specializing in border security, emergency management, transportation security, maritime security, and immigration enforcement is paramount. By investing in research and development, advocating for increased funding, and conducting comprehensive studies, we can ensure that our borders remain secure in the 21st century.

Data Analysis and Intelligence Sharing

In the fast-paced and interconnected world of the 21st century, border security has emerged as a critical concern for nations across the globe. With the ever-evolving nature of threats, it is essential for policymakers and security practitioners to adopt new approaches and technologies to ensure the safety and integrity of their borders. One such approach is data analysis and intelligence sharing, which has proved to be a game-changer in the field of border security.

Data analysis involves the systematic examination and interpretation of vast amounts of information collected from various sources. By leveraging the power of advanced analytics, governments can identify patterns, trends, and anomalies that may indicate potential threats to national security. This data-driven approach enables policymakers to make more informed decisions and allocate resources effectively.

Intelligence sharing plays a crucial role in enhancing border security. In an increasingly interconnected world, no single nation can tackle security challenges alone. By sharing intelligence with partner countries and international organizations, governments can gain a more comprehensive understanding of transnational threats and develop coordinated strategies to address them. This collaborative approach allows for the pooling of resources, expertise, and best practices, leading to enhanced border security outcomes.

For politicians, think tank scholars, professors, teachers, students, authors, and scholars interested in border security, data analysis and intelligence sharing offer invaluable insights and tools. By studying and understanding the potential of these approaches, stakeholders can contribute to the development of innovative policies and strategies that promote effective border security.

In the realm of emergency management, data analysis and intelligence sharing enable authorities to predict, prepare for, respond to, and recover from disasters more efficiently. By analyzing historical data and real-time information, emergency managers can identify areas prone to natural disasters, mobilize resources, and coordinate response efforts. Intelligence sharing among different agencies and jurisdictions ensures a coordinated and timely response to emergencies, minimizing loss of life and property.

Transportation security is another critical area where data analysis and intelligence sharing play a crucial role. By analyzing passenger data, cargo manifests, and other relevant information, governments can identify potential threats to aviation, rail, and road transportation systems. This proactive approach not only enhances the safety of travelers but also facilitates the smooth movement of goods and people across borders.

Maritime security is a particularly complex domain, given the vastness of the oceans and the multitude of actors involved. Data analysis and intelligence sharing enable maritime authorities to track vessels, monitor suspicious activities, and prevent piracy, smuggling, and other illicit activities. By collaborating and sharing information with international partners, countries can ensure the security of their territorial waters and maintain global maritime stability.

In the context of immigration enforcement, data analysis and intelligence sharing provide governments with valuable tools to manage migration flows effectively. By analyzing immigration patterns, authorities can identify high-risk individuals, detect fraudulent documents, and prevent illegal entry. Intelligence sharing among immigration agencies enables the exchange of information on individuals of interest, facilitating the identification and apprehension of criminals and terrorists.

In conclusion, data analysis and intelligence sharing have become indispensable tools in the field of border security. By harnessing the power of advanced analytics and collaborative information sharing, governments can enhance their ability to detect, prevent, and respond to threats in a rapidly evolving security landscape. For politicians, scholars, and practitioners interested in border security, understanding the potential of these approaches is essential for developing effective and innovative solutions that protect national interests and promote global security.

Chapter 9: The Role of Border Security in National Security

Border Security and Counterterrorism

In today's interconnected world, the issue of border security has taken on a new level of importance. As globalization continues to bring people and goods together from all corners of the globe, governments face unprecedented challenges in ensuring the safety and security of their nations. This subchapter, titled "Border Security and Counterterrorism," aims to provide a comprehensive analysis of the current landscape and offer potential solutions to address these challenges.

Border security plays a pivotal role in counterterrorism efforts. Terrorist organizations exploit weak borders and porous entry points to carry out their nefarious activities. The threat of terrorists infiltrating a country undetected is a constant concern for policymakers, making it imperative to design effective border security strategies.

This subchapter begins by examining the evolving nature of terrorism in the 21st century and its impact on border security. It delves into the tactics employed by terrorist groups, such as radicalization, recruitment, and the use of technology, that necessitate a more sophisticated approach to border control.

Furthermore, it explores the challenges faced by governments in balancing the need for robust security measures with the facilitation of legitimate trade and travel. Striking the right balance is crucial to avoid hindering economic growth and impeding the free movement of people while still ensuring national security.

The subchapter also delves into the role of technology in enhancing border security and counterterrorism efforts. It discusses the potential of advanced surveillance systems, biometric identification, and data analytics in strengthening border control. Additionally, it explores the importance of international collaboration and information sharing in combating transnational threats.

Moreover, this subchapter highlights the significance of emergency management, transportation security, maritime security, and immigration enforcement in the broader context of border security and counterterrorism. It emphasizes the need for a holistic approach that integrates these various fields to effectively address the multifaceted challenges posed by terrorism.

By providing a comprehensive analysis of the complex interplay between border security and counterterrorism, this subchapter aims to serve as a valuable resource for politicians, think tank scholars, professors, teachers, students, authors, and scholars. It offers insights into the current challenges faced by governments and provides potential solutions to enhance border security and counter terrorism efforts. With its focus on the niches of border security, emergency management, transportation security, maritime security, and immigration enforcement, it caters to the specific interests of these diverse audiences.

Border Security and Defense Strategies

In today's rapidly changing global landscape, the need for effective border security and defense strategies has become more crucial than ever before. As nations strive to protect their citizens, economies, and sovereignty, it is imperative to develop comprehensive approaches that address the multifaceted challenges faced in the 21st century. This subchapter delves into the intricacies of border security and defense strategies, offering valuable insights and solutions for politicians, think tank scholars, professors, teachers, students, authors, and scholars interested in the fields of border security, emergency management, transportation security, maritime security, and immigration enforcement.

The subchapter begins by examining the evolving nature of border security threats and the urgent need for innovative strategies to counter them. It explores the growing complexity of transnational crimes, terrorism, and illegal immigration, which demand a holistic approach that combines intelligence-sharing, robust technological solutions, and international cooperation. By understanding the dynamic nature of border security challenges, policymakers can develop effective defense strategies that safeguard national interests while promoting economic growth and cultural exchange.

Additionally, this subchapter highlights the importance of emergency management in border security. It explores the role of emergency response agencies in mitigating the impact of natural disasters, pandemics, and terrorist attacks at border regions. By integrating emergency management protocols into border security strategies, governments can enhance their preparedness and response capabilities, ensuring the safety and well-being of their citizens.

Furthermore, the subchapter delves into the realm of transportation security, emphasizing the need for robust measures to protect critical infrastructure, such as airports, seaports, and land transportation systems. It explores cutting-edge technologies, including biometrics, facial recognition, and advanced screening techniques, which can strengthen transportation security while facilitating legitimate travel and trade.

Maritime security is another critical aspect covered in this subchapter. With the increasing threats posed by piracy, smuggling, and illegal fishing, governments must develop strategies to safeguard their maritime borders and protect vital sea lanes. The subchapter discusses the importance of international cooperation, intelligence sharing, and maritime domain awareness in countering these threats effectively.

Lastly, the subchapter addresses the crucial issue of immigration enforcement. It explores the challenges associated with managing immigration flows, including border controls, visa policies, and deportation procedures. By adopting comprehensive immigration enforcement strategies that balance security concerns with humanitarian considerations, governments can effectively manage immigration while upholding human rights.

In conclusion, this subchapter provides a comprehensive overview of border security and defense strategies, offering valuable insights and solutions for policymakers, scholars, and professionals in the fields of border security, emergency management, transportation security, maritime security, and immigration enforcement. By understanding the dynamic nature of border security challenges and adopting innovative approaches, nations can safeguard their borders, protect their citizens, and promote economic prosperity in the 21st century.

Border Security and Economic Stability

In today's interconnected global economy, the issue of border security has far-reaching implications for economic stability. The challenges faced in this regard are multifaceted, requiring a comprehensive approach that addresses the complexities of the 21st-century landscape. This subchapter will delve into the intricate relationship between border security and economic stability, exploring the challenges and potential solutions.

Border security plays a vital role in maintaining economic stability by facilitating the smooth flow of goods, services, and people across national boundaries. Effective border management systems ensure the integrity of supply chains, supporting trade and investment, and fostering economic growth. Conversely, weak border security can have adverse effects on economic stability, as it enables illicit activities such as smuggling, human trafficking, and the movement of counterfeit goods, all of which undermine legitimate economic activities.

One of the key challenges in achieving border security and economic stability lies in striking a balance between facilitating legitimate trade and travel while detecting and deterring illicit activities. This requires the deployment of advanced technologies, intelligence-sharing mechanisms, and cooperation among nations. Politicians, think tank scholars, and professors have a crucial role to play in developing policies that promote efficient border management systems while minimizing disruptions to economic activities.

Furthermore, the subchapter will explore the significance of emergency management in the context of border security and economic stability. Natural disasters, pandemics, and other emergencies can severely impact border security and disrupt economic activities. Therefore, it is imperative to develop robust contingency plans and response mechanisms that account for these potential threats. Collaboration between government agencies, private sector stakeholders, and international partners is essential to effectively manage emergencies and maintain economic stability in the face of adversity.

Transportation security and maritime security are also intrinsically linked to border security and economic stability. The subchapter will delve into the challenges posed by the movement of people and goods through various modes of transportation, including land, air, and sea. It will explore the importance of implementing comprehensive security measures that encompass risk assessment, passenger and cargo screening, and the effective use of technology to safeguard critical transportation infrastructure.

Lastly, the subchapter will touch upon the role of immigration enforcement in maintaining border security and economic stability. A well-regulated immigration system that ensures the entry of skilled labor and contributes to the economy can positively impact economic stability. However, the subchapter will also highlight the challenges of managing unauthorized immigration and the need for effective enforcement measures that strike a balance between security concerns and economic realities.

In conclusion, the subchapter "Border Security and Economic Stability" highlights the intricate relationship between these two crucial aspects. It emphasizes the need for comprehensive strategies that address the challenges faced in border security while fostering economic stability. By engaging politicians, think tank scholars, professors, teachers, students, authors, and scholars, this subchapter aims to contribute to the dialogue surrounding border security, emergency management, transportation security, maritime security, and immigration enforcement, providing insights and potential solutions to these pressing issues.

Chapter 10: Future Trends and Innovations in Border Security

Emerging Technologies and their Impact

In this rapidly evolving world, emerging technologies have a profound impact on various aspects of society, including border security. As we step into the 21st century, it is crucial for policymakers, think tank scholars, professors, teachers, students, authors, and scholars to be aware of these technological advancements and their potential implications for border security, emergency management, transportation security, maritime security, and immigration enforcement.

One of the most significant emerging technologies is artificial intelligence (AI) and machine learning. These technologies have the potential to revolutionize border security by enhancing surveillance and threat detection capabilities. AI-powered systems can analyze vast amounts of data in real-time, identify patterns, and improve the accuracy and efficiency of border checks. Additionally, AI can help automate routine tasks, freeing up human resources to focus on more complex security challenges.

Another emerging technology with a significant impact is biometrics. Facial recognition, fingerprint scanning, and iris recognition technologies can be used to enhance border security by accurately verifying the identity of individuals entering or exiting a country. This technology can significantly improve immigration enforcement efforts and prevent identity theft or fraud.

Moreover, the Internet of Things (IoT) plays a crucial role in border security and emergency management. IoT-enabled devices can collect and transmit data in real-time, providing valuable insights for border patrol agents and emergency response teams. For example, smart sensors can detect unauthorized border crossings or monitor critical infrastructure, ensuring swift response to potential threats.

Furthermore, advancements in drone technology have transformed the way border security and maritime surveillance are conducted. Drones equipped with high-resolution cameras and thermal imaging sensors can cover vast areas quickly, providing real-time situational awareness and aiding in the detection of smuggling activities, illegal border crossings, or suspicious vessels.

Lastly, blockchain technology has the potential to revolutionize the management of immigration and border control systems. By leveraging the decentralized and immutable nature of blockchain, identity verification, visa processing, and immigration records can be securely stored, preventing fraud and improving efficiency.

In conclusion, emerging technologies have the power to significantly impact border security, emergency management, transportation security, maritime security, and immigration enforcement. Policymakers, scholars, and professionals in these niches must stay informed about the latest technological advancements to harness their potential benefits and address any associated challenges. By embracing these technologies responsibly, we can create a safer and more secure global environment.

International Cooperation and Information Sharing

In the fast-paced and interconnected world of the 21st century, the challenges faced by nations in securing their borders are more complex than ever before. Border security is not a standalone issue; it is intricately linked with emergency management, transportation security, maritime security, and immigration enforcement. To effectively address these challenges, international cooperation and information sharing are paramount.

Politicians, think tank scholars, professors, teachers, students, authors, and scholars involved in the realms of border security, emergency management, transportation security, maritime security, and immigration enforcement must recognize the significance of collaboration on a global scale. The threats faced by one nation often have ripple effects that can impact the entire international community. Therefore, it is imperative to foster mutual cooperation and exchange of information between nations.

International cooperation plays a vital role in tackling border security challenges. By joining forces, nations can pool their resources, knowledge, and expertise to develop comprehensive strategies that have a higher likelihood of success. Sharing best practices and lessons learned can help identify gaps in existing security measures and inspire innovative solutions. Through collaboration, nations can coordinate their efforts to detect and prevent the movement of illicit goods, human trafficking, and terrorist activities across borders.

Information sharing is the cornerstone of effective border security in the 21st century. Timely and accurate intelligence allows nations to anticipate threats, respond swiftly, and mitigate risks. Sharing intelligence on emerging threats, criminal networks, and suspicious activities not only enhances the ability to prevent security breaches but also facilitates the apprehension and prosecution of those involved. Furthermore, the exchange of information can aid in identifying patterns and trends, thereby enabling proactive measures to be taken.

To facilitate international cooperation and information sharing, platforms such as Interpol, Europol, and the United Nations play a crucial role. These organizations serve as conduits for collaboration, providing a framework for nations to exchange information, coordinate operations, and harmonize their approaches. Bilateral and multilateral agreements between countries further strengthen cooperation and foster trust among nations, enabling them to work together effectively.

In conclusion, the challenges faced in border security, emergency management, transportation security, maritime security, and immigration enforcement necessitate international cooperation and information sharing. Policymakers, scholars, and practitioners must recognize the interconnectedness of these issues and actively engage in collaborative efforts. By sharing expertise, resources, and intelligence, nations can enhance their border security measures and ensure the safety and well-being of their citizens. The 21st century demands a shift from isolated approaches to a global perspective, where countries work hand in hand to address the ever-evolving challenges in securing their borders.

Policy Recommendations for Enhancing Border Security

Introduction:

In an era of globalization, border security has become an increasingly critical concern for nations worldwide. This subchapter aims to provide comprehensive policy recommendations for enhancing border security, addressing the unique challenges faced by policymakers and stakeholders in the 21st century. With an audience encompassing politicians, think tank scholars, professors, teachers, students, authors, and scholars, these recommendations strive to offer practical solutions applicable to various niches, including border security, emergency management, transportation security, maritime security, and immigration enforcement.

1. Strengthening International Cooperation:

Collaboration among nations is paramount in combating cross-border threats. Governments should foster partnerships, information sharing, and joint operations to ensure a coordinated response to security challenges. Establishing and expanding international organizations dedicated to border security, such as Interpol, can facilitate effective collaboration and knowledge exchange between countries.

2. Technology and Infrastructure Investment:

Investing in advanced technology and infrastructure is crucial to fortify border security. Utilizing state-of-the-art surveillance systems, such as drones and satellite imaging, can enhance monitoring capabilities. Additionally, improving physical infrastructure at land, sea, and air entry points, including the deployment of biometric identification systems, can boost overall security measures.

3. Risk-Based Approach:

Implementing a risk-based approach allows authorities to allocate resources efficiently by focusing on high-risk individuals and goods. Utilizing advanced data analytics and intelligence to identify potential threats beforehand can enable border agencies to take proactive measures. By prioritizing resources based on risk assessment, border security agencies can more effectively detect and prevent illicit activities.

4. Enhanced Border Personnel Training:

Investing in comprehensive training programs for border personnel is vital. Training should encompass areas such as intelligence gathering, risk assessment, intercultural communication, and conflict resolution. Continuous professional development programs can ensure that border personnel remain up-to-date with evolving threats and possess the necessary skills to address them effectively.

5. Engaging Local Communities:

Engaging local communities can foster a sense of ownership and collaboration in border security. Governments should work with community leaders, educators, and civil society organizations to raise awareness about the importance of border security and encourage reporting of suspicious activities. This collaboration can help bridge the gap between authorities and communities, leading to more effective security outcomes.

Conclusion:

Enhancing border security requires a multifaceted approach that combines international cooperation, technology investment, risk-based strategies, personnel training, and community engagement. By implementing these policy recommendations, policymakers can strengthen border security in the 21st century, safeguarding nations from evolving threats while facilitating legitimate trade and travel. It is through collective efforts that we can achieve a more secure and interconnected world.

Conclusion: Addressing the Challenges and Building a Secure Future

In today's rapidly changing world, the issue of border security has become a top priority for nations across the globe. As highlighted throughout this book, the challenges we face in the 21st century are complex and multifaceted. However, by understanding and addressing these challenges head-on, we can build a secure future for our nations and protect the well-being of our citizens.

Border security is not a standalone issue; it intersects with various other domains such as emergency management, transportation security, maritime security, and immigration enforcement. As politicians, think tank scholars, professors, teachers, students, authors, and scholars, it is our collective responsibility to explore innovative solutions and strategies that can effectively address these challenges.

One of the key takeaways from this book is the need for collaboration and cooperation among nations. Border security is not a problem that can be solved by one country alone. Global challenges require global solutions. Policymakers should actively engage in bilateral and multilateral dialogues to share best practices, intelligence, and resources. By fostering international partnerships, we can enhance our collective ability to detect and deter threats at our borders.

Furthermore, investing in technology and research is crucial. The rapid advancement of technology presents both opportunities and challenges. Governments and relevant stakeholders should invest in cutting-edge technologies such as surveillance systems, biometrics, and data analytics. Additionally, fostering research and development in border security can lead to innovative solutions that are more efficient and cost-effective.

Education and training are also vital components of building a secure future. Governments should prioritize the training of border security personnel, equipping them with the necessary skills and knowledge to effectively address evolving threats. Additionally, public awareness campaigns can help educate citizens about the importance of border security and foster a sense of shared responsibility.

Lastly, it is essential to strike a balance between security and humanitarian considerations. While border security is crucial, it should not come at the expense of human rights and dignity. Policies should be designed to ensure the fair and humane treatment of individuals crossing borders, particularly vulnerable populations such as refugees and asylum seekers.

In conclusion, as we navigate the challenges of the 21st century, addressing border security requires a comprehensive and multi-faceted approach. By fostering international collaboration, embracing technology and research, investing in education and training, and upholding humanitarian values, we can build a secure future for our nations. As politicians, think tank scholars, professors, teachers, students, authors, and scholars, it is our collective responsibility to actively engage in this discourse and contribute to the development of effective solutions. Together, we can create a safer and more secure world for all.

References: List of Cited Sources

In this subchapter, we present a comprehensive list of cited sources that have been referenced throughout this book, "Border Security in the 21st Century: Challenges and Solutions." This compilation of reputable sources aims to provide our audience, consisting of politicians, think tank scholars, professors, teachers, students, authors, and scholars with a rich and diverse collection of materials to further their understanding of border security, emergency management, transportation security, maritime security, and immigration enforcement.

The references listed here have been carefully selected to cover a broad spectrum of topics related to border security. They include scholarly articles, books, reports, government documents, and research papers from authoritative sources. These materials have been written by renowned experts, academics, and practitioners from various fields, ensuring that our audience receives insights from multiple perspectives.

For those interested in the challenges and solutions surrounding border security, we have included references that explore the evolving nature of threats, such as terrorism, drug trafficking, and human smuggling. Additionally, we have included resources on the role of technology and intelligence in enhancing border security measures. These sources shed light on innovative strategies and best practices implemented globally to tackle these complex issues.

Emergency management is another critical aspect addressed in this book. The list of references provides a wealth of information on disaster preparedness, response, and recovery. These sources delve into the coordination efforts between multiple agencies, the importance of community engagement, and the integration of technology in emergency management systems.

Transportation security is a key concern in today's interconnected world. The references included in this section delve into the challenges faced in securing air, land, and sea transportation networks. They discuss the latest advancements in screening technologies, risk assessment methodologies, and the role of international cooperation in ensuring safe and secure travel.

The maritime security section covers a wide range of topics, including piracy, illegal fishing, and the protection of critical infrastructure in coastal regions. The cited sources provide insights into the legal frameworks governing maritime security, the role of navies and coast guards, and the challenges faced in securing vast oceanic spaces.

Lastly, immigration enforcement is a topic of great significance in border security discussions. The references in this section explore the policies, practices, and debates surrounding immigration enforcement efforts. They examine issues such as border control, asylum processing, detention centers, and the integration of migrants into host communities.

By providing this comprehensive list of cited sources, we hope to equip our audience with the necessary tools to delve deeper into the intricate and multifaceted issues of border security, emergency management, transportation security, maritime security, and immigration enforcement. These references serve as a valuable resource for politicians, think tank scholars, professors, teachers, students, authors, and scholars seeking to expand their knowledge and contribute to the ongoing discourse in these niches.